My Soul Journal

GLORY NELSON

BALBOA.PRESS
A DIVISION OF HAY HOUSE

Balboa Press books may be ordered through booksellers or by contacting:

Balboa Press
A Division of Hay House
1663 Liberty Drive
Bloomington, IN 47403
www.balboapress.com
844-682-1282

ISBN: 979-8-7652-2678-0 (sc)
ISBN: 979-8-7652-2679-7 (e)

Print information available on the last page.

Balboa Press rev. date: 04/08/2022

My Soul Journal

Welcome!

You are now one step closer to developing your daily soul practice! I am excited for you to start this amazing journey of self-exploration! Within these pages you will have opportunities to journal your dreams, thoughts, and passions. This practice will guide you to live a more authentic life.

Every morning, give yourself the gift of starting your day with intention and purpose. In the evening you will be guided to release the stresses of the day and have a restful sleep. Having a ritual like this will remind you of what is truly important in your life.

The Science Behind Journaling

Studies show that people who write in a journal have fewer stresses and are better at resolving conflicts. They also have a better sense of who they are and can sift through their thoughts and feelings much quicker than others. When you think or dream of a goal, you are activating your right-brain (your artistic side). When you write down your goal after you have the thought, you activate your left-brain (your logical side). When both parts of the brain are activated, it tells the rest of your body at a cellular level. It communicates strongly, I WANT THIS! The brain, body and the Universe then align with your soul's desire, creating a higher chance of your goals becoming a reality!

The Science Behind Gratitude

Research has shown that having a daily habit of gratitude improves physical and mental health. It enhances empathy and reduces aggression. People are happier and less likely to negative self-talk. When we keep a gratitude list, we get into a place of abundance which keeps us from focusing on the things we lack. We are also training the brain to think and express in a more positive way even when we are not dealing with gratitude. The more we practice gratitude in our lives, the more we realize that we have everything we need in that moment even when we are not feeling our best. This journal will become a treasure! Imagine a year from now, re-reading about your accomplishments, memories, maybe some struggles. It will showcase how far you've come, obstacles you overcame and cards that guided you through it. Social media shows us all the great times and memories we have had, but this journal will be a beautiful reminder of your dreams, thoughts, and overall journey.

Glory Nelson

How to use this journal

Morning

It is always important to **date** your journal pages. It's always fun to look back at dreams and what was currently happening in your life, to notice patterns and to watch the magic unfold.

Numerology is a system where each number carries its own frequency and meaning. To find the numerology for the day, which is called **Your Personal Day**, start by adding your birth month and day with the current month, day, and year. Ex. if your birth date is Jan 3rd and today is March 4, 2021, you will add 1 (month) + 3 (day) + 3 (current month) + 4 (current day) + 2+0+2+1 (current year) = 16, then reduce this until you get a single digit. 1 + 6 = 7. You are in a 7 vibration for the day. Based on the number meaning described below you will be in a day of contemplating, going within, resting, and dreaming.

Number Meanings

0   The infinite number, the zero has no end and no beginning. It is associated with the divine. And when it shows up with another number it is amplified. Ex. 30 is a 3 amplified by the Divine!

1   A new beginning, a new IDEA, birth, planting the seed, inspired thought. Assertive, leadership, pioneer, originality, independence

2   Balance or choice, union, weighing your options, duality, yin and yang, gatheringinformation for the IDEA. Sensitive, details, supportive, diplomatic

3   Creativity, the IDEA is being created, pregnant with life, Mother Nature, ready togive birth. Love, beauty, art, communication, social, joy

4   Structure, planning, foundation, container, the IDEA is born into the material world -practical, the one IDEA amplified by the Divine. Organizer, hard worker, responsible

5   Change and transformation, freedom, flexibility, traveling, movement, flow, the IDEA may need tweaking

6   Charity, giving and receiving, ebb and flow, giving from the heart, truth, kind, emotional, the IDEA can serve more than one purpose or person

7   Meditation, in7trospection, searching for spiritual truths, solitude, intuition. You need a break from the IDEA

8   Manifestation, seeing the bigger picture, as above so below, extrovert, The IDEA is alive and breathing and you are reaping the rewards

9   Humanitarian, brotherly love, universal love, completion of a cycle. The IDEA may take on a new life, it may be passed on, or may be done for good

Moon in: This is a great way to track our emotions and learn about astrology. As the astrological signs travel through the moon, it influences it. The moon influences the tides and since we are made up of mostly water, the moon affects us too. Working with the moon will teach us the best times to create and when to release. I suggest you download a moon app to track the moon and signs for the day. Ex. Moon in Leo -A dynamic and fiery sign. It is a good day to shine and take the lead.

Dream or Journal

Recording your dreams as soon as you wake up is a great way to start the day. Many times, we are so busy with daily life that we are unable to deal with looming issues. Getting to know your dreams and working with them can help. Dreams can give us all sorts of insights and ideas to help us live a better a life. If you don't remember your dream that morning, you can use this space to journal. Ask yourself a soul-searching question.

Example: How do I want to show up in my life today? What things do I really want to create for myself? Where do I see myself in a year from now?

My Cards for Today

This section invites you to ask for guidance and pull an affirmation, inspiration, oracle, or tarot card. This may assist you to get deeper insights on a question or a dream. I often find myself pulling one card off several decks and each card supports the other. Write down the name of the card and a small description. This is a magical way to begin your day.

Questions to ask the cards: What is my main message for today?

What did this part of my dream mean?

What should I focus on today?

Affirmation or Intention

This section will ensure that you start your day off in a positive and affirmative way. I find that the dream and the cards I pull, give me a good idea of what my intention should be for the day.

Example: "Today I will focus on being gentle with myself." You can be as creative with this as you want, but it should really reflect whatever way you are feeling that day and what you may be struggling with. For instance, if you are struggling with controlling a situation, then your affirmation may be, "I lovingly allow myself to go

with the flow and I will love every minute of it!" Remember to state your intention in a positive way, then read it out loud.

Today I will feed my soul

This part is so essential. I personally struggle with this one. Before you begin working with this journal, it may be wise to write down all the things that feed your soul, all the things that bring you joy, make you smile or warms your heart. For me, it's playing music or sitting with a warm cup of coffee and cuddling up with a blanket. Some people like salt baths, walking their dog, meditating, singing, talking with a friend. Whatever it may be for you, find one small thing that will feed your soul today. This allows us to practice self-care which is essential for our well-being.

I will work on these chakras and colors today

We all have seven chakras in the body. Chakras are energy centers. There are many books on chakras that go in depth with each energy point, but for our quick daily soul practice we will keep it simple and fun. Each chakra has a corresponding color and meaning. In this section, you will get in tune with what chakra you should be working with based on the words and thoughts you have already recorded. Your dreams, your intention, your cards will all be indicators of which chakra you should pay attention to today.

Example: If my dreams are about speaking up for myself, and the cards I get are all about expression, then I may want to work with the "Throat Chakra" and wear blue. We are often called to work with more than one chakra. There is no wrong way of doing this. You may want to wear the color of the chakra and/or you may want to eat foods of that same color to align with the power of that chakra.

Root Chakra – Red

This is your base chakra, located at the base of your spine. This chakra is all about the physical world, survival, childhood, family, ancestral, earthy, and grounding. This chakra has to do with money, safety, your everyday life. Negative aspect – fear.

Sacral Chakra – Orange

It is located right below the naval. This chakra is associated with creativity, sexual energy, sensuality, feelings, pleasure, motivation. Negative aspect – guilt.

Solar Plexus – Yellow

This is located above your naval. This chakra is associated with power, action, intuition, strength, energy (think of the sun) ego. Negative aspect – Shame.

Heart – Green or Pink

It is located near the heart. This chakra is associated with love, emotions, relationships, service, self-love, peace, gratefulness. Negative aspect – Grief.

Throat – Blue

It is located near the throat area. This chakra is all about communication, expression, breathing, speaking, your truth, messages, vibrations. Negative aspects – Lies

3rd Eye – Indigo

It is located right above the eyes. This chakra is associated with psychic abilities, dreams, visions, imagination, the 6th sense. Negative aspect – Illusion

Crown – Violet

It is located right above your head. This chakra is all about our connection to the divine, enlightenment, awakening, wisdom, The Universe, Spirit, God.

Evening

One thing I loved about today

This allows you to find that one thing you loved about your day. Feel free to write more than one, I dare you! This a good time to pat yourself on the back about an accomplishment and to remember that celebrating in small ways is a good habit to create. I love this section because this allows me to focus on something positive and good to look forward to. We often start dreading the next day because of X, Y, and Z. Let's turn that around! There is no reason to worry about something that hasn't even happened yet.

This happened today

This is the section where you journal about your day, specific experiences, memories, something funny your friend said. You can vent about the argument you had; it is better to write it down on paper than to keep it bottled up. This section is just for you! Ex. After work, a group of us went to see a movie, we had a blast. I love the little dessert place we went to afterwards. Sometimes I think this is an extremely important section. If you find yourself writing the same things, for example, I had another argument with my spouse, this section will start showing you patterns within yourself and others.

Insights, Lessons and Synchronicity

Write down any insights or lessons that came up for you. What stood out? I truly believe that the Universe is speaking to us constantly through signs, animals, the radio, dreams, books, symbols and emails. A synchronicity is a coincidence with meaning. When something looks out of the ordinary, pay attention to it. If a squirrel keeps following you on your walk, it means something.

Ex: If three people have mentioned the same book in one week, it's a synchronicity, or the Universe nudging you to read the book. The answer you have been looking for may be in chapter two. Write these down and you may just start seeing a beautiful intricate correspondence between you and the Universe.

Today I am grateful

In the welcome page, we went over why it is important to keep a gratitude list. In the beginning you will be grateful for all the obvious things we are supposed to be grateful for, like our family, our job, our home etc.… Further into this practice, you will find yourself writing things like, "I am grateful for the energy I had today, I was able to get so much stuff done.", or "I am grateful for the letter I received today, it meant so much to me." You will be grateful for the biggest and smallest things, and this encourages us to look deeper at the meaningful things in our lives daily.

Quick to do list

This one is my favorite! You know that moment when you lay your head down to go to sleep and suddenly you realize you forgot to pick up the dry cleaning, or you forgot to make that appointment? You start thinking of all the things you need to do tomorrow, and sleep seems like the last thing on your mind. Well now you can write it down here, leave your worries on the page and drift off to dream land. Happy Dreaming!

Morning

Date: _____

Numerology: _____

Moon in: _____

Dream or Journal:

_____
_____
_____
_____
_____
_____
_____
_____
_____
_____
_____

My cards for today are...

_____
_____
_____
_____

Affirmations, Intentions, or Wishes for today...

_____
_____

Today, I will feed my soul by...

_____
_____

I will work with these Chakras and colors today...

_____
_____

Evening

One thing I loved about today was:

_____

_____

I am so excited for tomorrow because...

_____

_____

This happened today...

_____

_____

_____

_____

_____

Insights, lessons, and synchronicities of the day...

_____

_____

_____

Today I am grateful for...

1. _____   5. _____
2. _____   6. _____
3. _____   7. _____
4. _____   8. _____

Quick To-Do list for tomorrow:

1. _____   5. _____
2. _____   6. _____
3. _____   7. _____
4. _____   8. _____

Morning

Date: _____

Numerology: _____

Moon in: _____

Dream or Journal:

_____

_____

_____

_____

_____

_____

_____

_____

_____

_____

_____

My cards for today are...

_____

_____

_____

_____

Affirmations, Intentions, or Wishes for today...

_____

_____

Today, I will feed my soul by...

_____

_____

I will work with these Chakras and colors today...

_____

_____

Evening

One thing I loved about today was:

_____

_____

I am so excited for tomorrow because...

_____

_____

This happened today...

_____

_____

_____

_____

_____

Insights, lessons, and synchronicities of the day...

_____

_____

_____

Today I am grateful for...

1. _____   5. _____
2. _____   6. _____
3. _____   7. _____
4. _____   8. _____

Quick To-Do list for tomorrow:

1. _____   5. _____
2. _____   6. _____
3. _____   7. _____
4. _____   8. _____

Morning

Date: _____

Numerology: _____

Moon in: _____

Dream or Journal:

_____
_____
_____
_____
_____
_____
_____
_____
_____
_____
_____

My cards for today are...

_____
_____
_____
_____

Affirmations, Intentions, or Wishes for today...

_____
_____

Today, I will feed my soul by...

_____
_____

I will work with these Chakras and colors today...

_____
_____

Evening

One thing I loved about today was:

_____

_____

I am so excited for tomorrow because...

_____

_____

This happened today...

_____

_____

_____

_____

_____

Insights, lessons, and synchronicities of the day...

_____

_____

_____

Today I am grateful for...

1. _____ 5. _____
2. _____ 6. _____
3. _____ 7. _____
4. _____ 8. _____

Quick To-Do list for tomorrow:

1. _____ 5. _____
2. _____ 6. _____
3. _____ 7. _____
4. _____ 8. _____

Morning

Date: _____

Numerology: _____

Moon in: _____

Dream or Journal:

_____

_____

_____

_____

_____

_____

_____

_____

_____

_____

_____

My cards for today are...

_____

_____

_____

_____

Affirmations, Intentions, or Wishes for today...

_____

_____

Today, I will feed my soul by...

_____

_____

I will work with these Chakras and colors today...

_____

_____

Evening

One thing I loved about today was:

_____

_____

I am so excited for tomorrow because...

_____

_____

This happened today...

_____

_____

_____

_____

_____

Insights, lessons, and synchronicities of the day...

_____

_____

_____

Today I am grateful for...

1. _____   5. _____
2. _____   6. _____
3. _____   7. _____
4. _____   8. _____

Quick To-Do list for tomorrow:

1. _____   5. _____
2. _____   6. _____
3. _____   7. _____
4. _____   8. _____

Morning

Date: _____

Numerology: _____

Moon in: _____

Dream or Journal:

_____

_____

_____

_____

_____

_____

_____

_____

_____

_____

_____

My cards for today are...

_____

_____

_____

_____

Affirmations, Intentions, or Wishes for today...

_____

_____

Today, I will feed my soul by...

_____

_____

I will work with these Chakras and colors today...

_____

_____

One thing I loved about today was:

_____
_____

I am so excited for tomorrow because...

_____
_____

This happened today...

_____
_____
_____
_____
_____
_____

Insights, lessons, and synchronicities of the day...

_____
_____
_____

Today I am grateful for...

1. _____   5. _____
2. _____   6. _____
3. _____   7. _____
4. _____   8. _____

Quick To-Do list for tomorrow:

1. _____   5. _____
2. _____   6. _____
3. _____   7. _____
4. _____   8. _____

Morning

Date: _____

Numerology: _____

Moon in: _____

Dream or Journal:

_____

_____

_____

_____

_____

_____

_____

_____

_____

_____

_____

My cards for today are...

_____

_____

_____

_____

_____

Affirmations, Intentions, or Wishes for today...

_____

_____

Today, I will feed my soul by...

_____

_____

I will work with these Chakras and colors today...

_____

_____

Evening

One thing I loved about today was:

_____
_____

I am so excited for tomorrow because...

_____
_____

This happened today...

_____
_____
_____
_____
_____

Insights, lessons, and synchronicities of the day...

_____
_____
_____

Today I am grateful for...

1. _____   5. _____
2. _____   6. _____
3. _____   7. _____
4. _____   8. _____

Quick To-Do list for tomorrow:

1. _____   5. _____
2. _____   6. _____
3. _____   7. _____
4. _____   8. _____

Morning

Date: _____

Numerology: _____

Moon in: _____

Dream or Journal:

_____

_____

_____

_____

_____

_____

_____

_____

_____

_____

My cards for today are...

_____

_____

_____

_____

Affirmations, Intentions, or Wishes for today...

_____

_____

Today, I will feed my soul by...

_____

_____

I will work with these Chakras and colors today...

_____

_____

Evening

One thing I loved about today was:

_____

_____

I am so excited for tomorrow because...

_____

_____

This happened today...

_____

_____

_____

_____

_____

Insights, lessons, and synchronicities of the day...

_____

_____

_____

Today I am grateful for...

1. _____   5. _____
2. _____   6. _____
3. _____   7. _____
4. _____   8. _____

Quick To-Do list for tomorrow:

1. _____   5. _____
2. _____   6. _____
3. _____   7. _____
4. _____   8. _____

Morning

Date: _____

Numerology: _____

Moon in: _____

Dream or Journal:

_____
_____
_____
_____
_____
_____
_____
_____
_____
_____
_____
_____

My cards for today are...

_____
_____
_____
_____

Affirmations, Intentions, or Wishes for today...

_____
_____

Today, I will feed my soul by...

_____
_____

I will work with these Chakras and colors today...

_____
_____

Evening

One thing I loved about today was:

_____

_____

I am so excited for tomorrow because...

_____

_____

This happened today...

_____

_____

_____

_____

_____

Insights, lessons, and synchronicities of the day...

_____

_____

_____

Today I am grateful for...

1. _____   5. _____
2. _____   6. _____
3. _____   7. _____
4. _____   8. _____

Quick To-Do list for tomorrow:

1. _____   5. _____
2. _____   6. _____
3. _____   7. _____
4. _____   8. _____

Morning

Date: _____

Numerology: _____

Moon in: _____

Dream or Journal:

_____
_____
_____
_____
_____
_____
_____
_____
_____
_____

My cards for today are...

_____
_____
_____
_____

Affirmations, Intentions, or Wishes for today...

_____
_____

Today, I will feed my soul by...

_____
_____

I will work with these Chakras and colors today...

_____
_____

Evening

One thing I loved about today was:

_____

_____

I am so excited for tomorrow because...

_____

_____

This happened today...

_____

_____

_____

_____

_____

Insights, lessons, and synchronicities of the day...

_____

_____

_____

Today I am grateful for...

1. _____   5. _____
2. _____   6. _____
3. _____   7. _____
4. _____   8. _____

Quick To-Do list for tomorrow:

1. _____   5. _____
2. _____   6. _____
3. _____   7. _____
4. _____   8. _____

Morning

Date: _____

Numerology: _____

Moon in: _____

Dream or Journal:

_____
_____
_____
_____
_____
_____
_____
_____
_____
_____

My cards for today are…

_____
_____
_____
_____

Affirmations, Intentions, or Wishes for today...

_____
_____

Today, I will feed my soul by...

_____
_____

I will work with these Chakras and colors today...

_____
_____

Evening

One thing I loved about today was:

_____

_____

I am so excited for tomorrow because...

_____

_____

This happened today...

_____

_____

_____

_____

_____

_____

Insights, lessons, and synchronicities of the day...

_____

_____

_____

_____

Today I am grateful for...

1. _____   5. _____
2. _____   6. _____
3. _____   7. _____
4. _____   8. _____

Quick To-Do list for tomorrow:

1. _____   5. _____
2. _____   6. _____
3. _____   7. _____
4. _____   8. _____

Morning

Date: _____

Numerology: _____

Moon in: _____

Dream or Journal:

_____

_____

_____

_____

_____

_____

_____

_____

_____

My cards for today are...

_____

_____

_____

_____

Affirmations, Intentions, or Wishes for today...

_____

_____

Today, I will feed my soul by...

_____

_____

I will work with these Chakras and colors today...

_____

_____

Evening

One thing I loved about today was:

_____
_____

I am so excited for tomorrow because...

_____
_____

This happened today...

_____
_____
_____
_____
_____
_____

Insights, lessons, and synchronicities of the day...

_____
_____
_____

Today I am grateful for...

1. _____   5. _____
2. _____   6. _____
3. _____   7. _____
4. _____   8. _____

Quick To-Do list for tomorrow:

1. _____   5. _____
2. _____   6. _____
3. _____   7. _____
4. _____   8. _____

Morning

Date: _____

Numerology: _____

Moon in: _____

Dream or Journal:

_____
_____
_____
_____
_____
_____
_____
_____
_____
_____
_____

My cards for today are...

_____
_____
_____
_____

Affirmations, Intentions, or Wishes for today...

_____
_____

Today, I will feed my soul by...

_____
_____

I will work with these Chakras and colors today...

_____
_____

Evening

One thing I loved about today was:

_____

_____

I am so excited for tomorrow because...

_____

_____

This happened today...

_____

_____

_____

_____

_____

Insights, lessons, and synchronicities of the day...

_____

_____

_____

Today I am grateful for...

1. _____   5. _____
2. _____   6. _____
3. _____   7. _____
4. _____   8. _____

Quick To-Do list for tomorrow:

1. _____   5. _____
2. _____   6. _____
3. _____   7. _____
4. _____   8. _____

Morning

Date: _____

Numerology: _____

Moon in: _____

Dream or Journal:

_____
_____
_____
_____
_____
_____
_____
_____
_____
_____

My cards for today are...

_____
_____
_____
_____

Affirmations, Intentions, or Wishes for today...

_____
_____

Today, I will feed my soul by...

_____
_____

I will work with these Chakras and colors today...

_____
_____

Evening

One thing I loved about today was:

_____

_____

I am so excited for tomorrow because...

_____

_____

This happened today...

_____

_____

_____

_____

_____

_____

Insights, lessons, and synchronicities of the day...

_____

_____

_____

Today I am grateful for...

1. _____   5. _____
2. _____   6. _____
3. _____   7. _____
4. _____   8. _____

Quick To-Do list for tomorrow:

1. _____   5. _____
2. _____   6. _____
3. _____   7. _____
4. _____   8. _____

Morning

Date: _____

Numerology: _____

Moon in: _____

Dream or Journal:

_____
_____
_____
_____
_____
_____
_____
_____
_____
_____
_____

My cards for today are...

_____
_____
_____
_____

Affirmations, Intentions, or Wishes for today...

_____
_____

Today, I will feed my soul by...

_____
_____

I will work with these Chakras and colors today...

_____
_____

One thing I loved about today was:

_____

_____

I am so excited for tomorrow because...

_____

_____

This happened today...

_____

_____

_____

_____

_____

Insights, lessons, and synchronicities of the day...

_____

_____

_____

Today I am grateful for...

1. _____   5. _____
2. _____   6. _____
3. _____   7. _____
4. _____   8. _____

Quick To-Do list for tomorrow:

1. _____   5. _____
2. _____   6. _____
3. _____   7. _____
4. _____   8. _____

Morning

Date: _____

Numerology: _____

Moon in: _____

Dream or Journal:

_____

_____

_____

_____

_____

_____

_____

_____

_____

_____

My cards for today are...

_____

_____

_____

_____

Affirmations, Intentions, or Wishes for today...

_____

_____

Today, I will feed my soul by...

_____

_____

I will work with these Chakras and colors today...

_____

_____

Evening

One thing I loved about today was:

_____

_____

I am so excited for tomorrow because...

_____

_____

This happened today...

_____

_____

_____

_____

_____

Insights, lessons, and synchronicities of the day...

_____

_____

_____

Today I am grateful for...

1. _____   5. _____
2. _____   6. _____
3. _____   7. _____
4. _____   8. _____

Quick To-Do list for tomorrow:

1. _____   5. _____
2. _____   6. _____
3. _____   7. _____
4. _____   8. _____

Morning

Date: _____

Numerology: _____

Moon in: _____

Dream or Journal:

_____
_____
_____
_____
_____
_____
_____
_____
_____
_____

My cards for today are...

_____
_____
_____
_____

Affirmations, Intentions, or Wishes for today...

_____
_____

Today, I will feed my soul by...

_____
_____

I will work with these Chakras and colors today...

_____
_____

Evening

One thing I loved about today was:

_____

_____

I am so excited for tomorrow because...

_____

_____

This happened today...

_____

_____

_____

_____

_____

Insights, lessons, and synchronicities of the day...

_____

_____

_____

Today I am grateful for...

1. _____   5. _____
2. _____   6. _____
3. _____   7. _____
4. _____   8. _____

Quick To-Do list for tomorrow:

1. _____   5. _____
2. _____   6. _____
3. _____   7. _____
4. _____   8. _____

Morning

Date: _____

Numerology: _____

Moon in: _____

Dream or Journal:

_____
_____
_____
_____
_____
_____
_____
_____
_____
_____
_____

My cards for today are...

_____
_____
_____
_____

Affirmations, Intentions, or Wishes for today...

_____
_____

Today, I will feed my soul by...

_____
_____

I will work with these Chakras and colors today...

_____
_____

Evening

One thing I loved about today was:

_____
_____

I am so excited for tomorrow because...

_____
_____

This happened today...

_____
_____
_____
_____
_____
_____

Insights, lessons, and synchronicities of the day...

_____
_____
_____

Today I am grateful for...

1. _____   5. _____
2. _____   6. _____
3. _____   7. _____
4. _____   8. _____

Quick To-Do list for tomorrow:

1. _____   5. _____
2. _____   6. _____
3. _____   7. _____
4. _____   8. _____

Morning

Date: _____

Numerology: _____

Moon in: _____

Dream or Journal:

_____
_____
_____
_____
_____
_____
_____
_____
_____

My cards for today are...

_____
_____
_____
_____

Affirmations, Intentions, or Wishes for today...

_____
_____

Today, I will feed my soul by...

_____
_____

I will work with these Chakras and colors today...

_____
_____

Evening

One thing I loved about today was:

_____

_____

I am so excited for tomorrow because...

_____

_____

This happened today...

_____

_____

_____

_____

_____

Insights, lessons, and synchronicities of the day...

_____

_____

_____

Today I am grateful for...

1. _____   5. _____
2. _____   6. _____
3. _____   7. _____
4. _____   8. _____

Quick To-Do list for tomorrow:

1. _____   5. _____
2. _____   6. _____
3. _____   7. _____
4. _____   8. _____

Morning

Date: _____

Numerology: _____

Moon in: _____

Dream or Journal:

_____
_____
_____
_____
_____
_____
_____
_____
_____
_____
_____

My cards for today are...

_____
_____
_____
_____

Affirmations, Intentions, or Wishes for today...

_____
_____

Today, I will feed my soul by...

_____
_____

I will work with these Chakras and colors today...

_____
_____

Evening

One thing I loved about today was:

_____

_____

I am so excited for tomorrow because...

_____

_____

This happened today...

_____

_____

_____

_____

_____

Insights, lessons, and synchronicities of the day...

_____

_____

_____

Today I am grateful for...

1. _____   5. _____
2. _____   6. _____
3. _____   7. _____
4. _____   8. _____

Quick To-Do list for tomorrow:

1. _____   5. _____
2. _____   6. _____
3. _____   7. _____
4. _____   8. _____

Morning

Dream or Journal:

_____

_____

_____

_____

_____

_____

_____

_____

_____

_____

My cards for today are...

_____

_____

_____

Affirmations, Intentions, or Wishes for today...

_____

_____

Today, I will feed my soul by...

_____

_____

I will work with these Chakras and colors today...

_____

_____

One thing I loved about today was:

_____

_____

I am so excited for tomorrow because…

_____

_____

This happened today…

_____

_____

_____

_____

_____

Insights, lessons, and synchronicities of the day…

_____

_____

_____

Today I am grateful for…

1. _____   5. _____
2. _____   6. _____
3. _____   7. _____
4. _____   8. _____

Quick To-Do list for tomorrow:

1. _____   5. _____
2. _____   6. _____
3. _____   7. _____
4. _____   8. _____

Morning

Date: _____

Numerology: _____

Moon in: _____

Dream or Journal:

_____
_____
_____
_____
_____
_____
_____
_____
_____
_____
_____

My cards for today are...

_____
_____
_____
_____

Affirmations, Intentions, or Wishes for today...

_____
_____

Today, I will feed my soul by...

_____
_____

I will work with these Chakras and colors today...

_____
_____

Evening

One thing I loved about today was:

_____

_____

I am so excited for tomorrow because...

_____

_____

This happened today...

_____

_____

_____

_____

_____

Insights, lessons, and synchronicities of the day...

_____

_____

_____

Today I am grateful for...

1. _____   5. _____
2. _____   6. _____
3. _____   7. _____
4. _____   8. _____

Quick To-Do list for tomorrow:

1. _____   5. _____
2. _____   6. _____
3. _____   7. _____
4. _____   8. _____

Morning

Date: _____

Numerology: _____

Moon in: _____

Dream or Journal:

_____

_____

_____

_____

_____

_____

_____

_____

_____

_____

_____

My cards for today are...

_____

_____

_____

_____

Affirmations, Intentions, or Wishes for today...

_____

_____

Today, I will feed my soul by...

_____

_____

I will work with these Chakras and colors today...

_____

_____

Evening

One thing I loved about today was:

_____

_____

I am so excited for tomorrow because...

_____

_____

This happened today...

_____

_____

_____

_____

_____

Insights, lessons, and synchronicities of the day...

_____

_____

_____

Today I am grateful for...

1. _____   5. _____
2. _____   6. _____
3. _____   7. _____
4. _____   8. _____

Quick To-Do list for tomorrow:

1. _____   5. _____
2. _____   6. _____
3. _____   7. _____
4. _____   8. _____

Morning

Date: _____

Numerology: _____

Moon in: _____

Dream or Journal:

_____

_____

_____

_____

_____

_____

_____

_____

_____

_____

My cards for today are...

_____

_____

_____

_____

Affirmations, Intentions, or Wishes for today...

_____

_____

Today, I will feed my soul by...

_____

_____

I will work with these Chakras and colors today...

_____

_____

One thing I loved about today was:

_____

_____

I am so excited for tomorrow because...

_____

_____

This happened today...

_____

_____

_____

_____

_____

Insights, lessons, and synchronicities of the day...

_____

_____

_____

Today I am grateful for...

1. _____   5. _____
2. _____   6. _____
3. _____   7. _____
4. _____   8. _____

Quick To-Do list for tomorrow:

1. _____   5. _____
2. _____   6. _____
3. _____   7. _____
4. _____   8. _____

Morning

Date: _____

Numerology: _____

Moon in: _____

Dream or Journal:

_____

_____

_____

_____

_____

_____

_____

_____

_____

_____

My cards for today are...

_____

_____

_____

_____

Affirmations, Intentions, or Wishes for today...

_____

_____

Today, I will feed my soul by...

_____

_____

I will work with these Chakras and colors today...

_____

_____

Evening

One thing I loved about today was:

_____

_____

I am so excited for tomorrow because...

_____

_____

This happened today...

_____

_____

_____

_____

_____

Insights, lessons, and synchronicities of the day...

_____

_____

_____

Today I am grateful for...

1. _____   5. _____
2. _____   6. _____
3. _____   7. _____
4. _____   8. _____

Quick To-Do list for tomorrow:

1. _____   5. _____
2. _____   6. _____
3. _____   7. _____
4. _____   8. _____

Morning

Date: _____

Numerology: _____

Moon in: _____

Dream or Journal:

_____
_____
_____
_____
_____
_____
_____
_____
_____

My cards for today are...

_____
_____
_____
_____

Affirmations, Intentions, or Wishes for today...

_____
_____

Today, I will feed my soul by...

_____
_____

I will work with these Chakras and colors today...

_____
_____

Evening

One thing I loved about today was:

_____
_____

I am so excited for tomorrow because...

_____
_____

This happened today...

_____
_____
_____
_____
_____

Insights, lessons, and synchronicities of the day...

_____
_____
_____

Today I am grateful for...

1. _____   5. _____
2. _____   6. _____
3. _____   7. _____
4. _____   8. _____

Quick To-Do list for tomorrow:

1. _____   5. _____
2. _____   6. _____
3. _____   7. _____
4. _____   8. _____

Morning

Date: _____

Numerology: _____

Moon in: _____

Dream or Journal:

_____

_____

_____

_____

_____

_____

_____

_____

_____

_____

_____

My cards for today are...

_____

_____

_____

_____

Affirmations, Intentions, or Wishes for today...

_____

_____

Today, I will feed my soul by...

_____

_____

I will work with these Chakras and colors today...

_____

_____

Evening

One thing I loved about today was:

_____

_____

I am so excited for tomorrow because...

_____

_____

This happened today...

_____

_____

_____

_____

_____

Insights, lessons, and synchronicities of the day...

_____

_____

_____

Today I am grateful for...

1. _____   5. _____
2. _____   6. _____
3. _____   7. _____
4. _____   8. _____

Quick To-Do list for tomorrow:

1. _____   5. _____
2. _____   6. _____
3. _____   7. _____
4. _____   8. _____

Morning

Date: _____

Numerology: _____

Moon in: _____

Dream or Journal:

_____
_____
_____
_____
_____
_____
_____
_____
_____
_____
_____

My cards for today are...

_____
_____
_____
_____

Affirmations, Intentions, or Wishes for today...

_____
_____

Today, I will feed my soul by...

_____
_____

I will work with these Chakras and colors today...

_____
_____

Evening

One thing I loved about today was:

_____

_____

I am so excited for tomorrow because...

_____

_____

This happened today...

_____

_____

_____

_____

_____

Insights, lessons, and synchronicities of the day...

_____

_____

_____

Today I am grateful for...

1. _____   5. _____

2. _____   6. _____

3. _____   7. _____

4. _____   8. _____

Quick To-Do list for tomorrow:

1. _____   5. _____

2. _____   6. _____

3. _____   7. _____

4. _____   8. _____

Morning

Date: _____

Numerology: _____

Moon in: _____

Dream or Journal:

_____
_____
_____
_____
_____
_____
_____
_____
_____
_____

My cards for today are...

_____
_____
_____

Affirmations, Intentions, or Wishes for today...

_____
_____

Today, I will feed my soul by...

_____
_____

I will work with these Chakras and colors today...

_____
_____

Evening

One thing I loved about today was:

_____

_____

I am so excited for tomorrow because...

_____

_____

This happened today...

_____

_____

_____

_____

_____

Insights, lessons, and synchronicities of the day...

_____

_____

_____

Today I am grateful for...

1. _____   5. _____
2. _____   6. _____
3. _____   7. _____
4. _____   8. _____

Quick To-Do list for tomorrow:

1. _____   5. _____
2. _____   6. _____
3. _____   7. _____
4. _____   8. _____

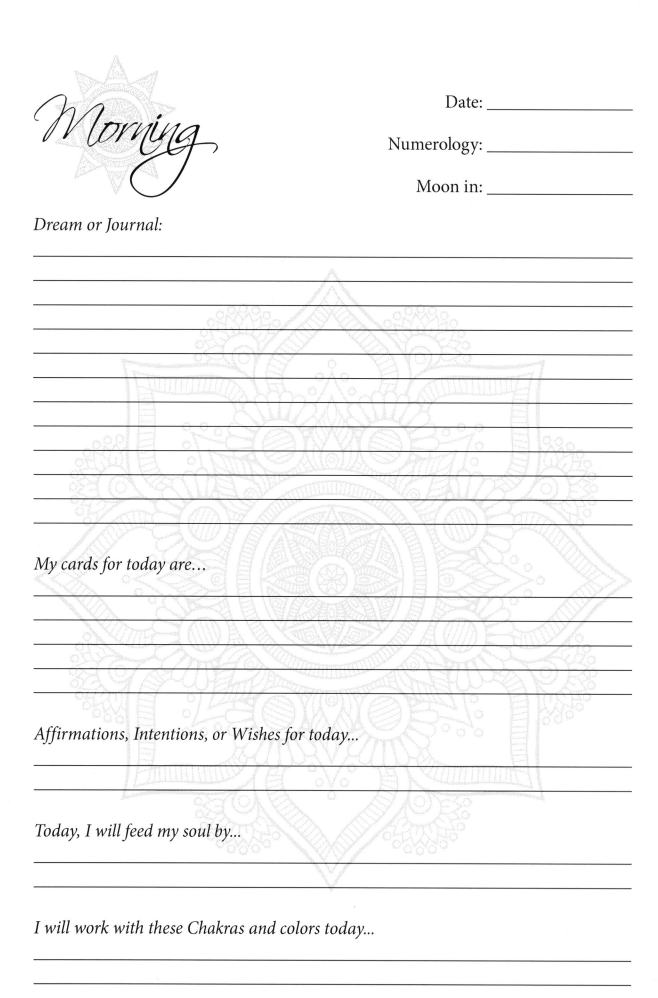

Morning

Date: _____

Numerology: _____

Moon in: _____

Dream or Journal:

_____
_____
_____
_____
_____
_____
_____
_____
_____
_____
_____

My cards for today are...

_____
_____
_____
_____

Affirmations, Intentions, or Wishes for today...

_____
_____

Today, I will feed my soul by...

_____
_____

I will work with these Chakras and colors today...

_____
_____

Evening

One thing I loved about today was:

_____

_____

I am so excited for tomorrow because…

_____

_____

This happened today…

_____

_____

_____

_____

_____

Insights, lessons, and synchronicities of the day…

_____

_____

_____

Today I am grateful for…

1. _____   5. _____
2. _____   6. _____
3. _____   7. _____
4. _____   8. _____

Quick To-Do list for tomorrow:

1. _____   5. _____
2. _____   6. _____
3. _____   7. _____
4. _____   8. _____

Morning

Date: _____

Numerology: _____

Moon in: _____

Dream or Journal:

_____
_____
_____
_____
_____
_____
_____
_____
_____
_____

My cards for today are...

_____
_____
_____
_____

Affirmations, Intentions, or Wishes for today...

_____
_____

Today, I will feed my soul by...

_____
_____

I will work with these Chakras and colors today...

_____
_____

One thing I loved about today was:

_____

_____

I am so excited for tomorrow because...

_____

_____

This happened today...

_____

_____

_____

_____

_____

Insights, lessons, and synchronicities of the day...

_____

_____

_____

Today I am grateful for...

1. _____   5. _____

2. _____   6. _____

3. _____   7. _____

4. _____   8. _____

Quick To-Do list for tomorrow:

1. _____   5. _____

2. _____   6. _____

3. _____   7. _____

4. _____   8. _____

Resources

I suggest you download a Numerology app and a Moon app. I use Numerology by Miromax and iLuna by Sirius Lab

My favorite Tarot Decks:

The Rider Waite Psychic Tarot by John Holland
Osho Zen Tarot
The Robin Wood Deck

My favorite Oracle Decks:

The Sacred Traveler by Dense Linn
The Mystical Shaman Oracle by Baron-Reid, Villoldo, Lobos
Dream Oracle Card by Kelly Sullivan Walden
Rumi Oracle by Alana Fairchild

Books about the Moon:

Lunar Abundance by Ezzie Spencer
Moonology by Yasmin Boland

Books about dreams:

Go to my website - www.glorynelson.com

Printed in the United States
by Baker & Taylor Publisher Services